SING
TO
THE
SUN

POEMS AND PICTURES BY ASHLEY BRYAN

SING
TO
THE
SUN

HarperCollinsPublishers

Sing to the Sun
Copyright © 1992 by Ashley Bryan
Printed in the U.S.A.   All rights reserved.
Typography by Al Cetta
1   2   3   4   5   6   7   8   9   10
First Edition

Library of Congress Cataloging-in-Publication Data
Bryan, Ashley.
   Sing to the sun : poems and pictures / by Ashley Bryan.
      p.   cm.
   Summary: A collection of poems and paintings celebrating the ups and
downs of life.
   ISBN 0-06-020829-5. — ISBN 0-06-020833-3 (lib. bdg.)
   1. Children's poetry, American.   [1. American poetry.]   I. Title.
PS3552.R848S57   1992   91-38359
811' .54—dc20   CIP
                                                                AC

For Tena Bowlay Williams
and
To the memory of my sister
Emerald

SONG

Sing to the sun
It will listen
And warm your words
Your joy will rise
Like the sun
And glow
Within you

Sing to the moon
It will hear
And soothe your cares
Your fears will set
Like the moon
And fade
Within you

SWEET TALK

Maribelle was dark as cloves
Marigold, cocoa brown
One morning, early, both arose
And tiptoed into town

Maribelle was dressed in green
Marigold wore yellow
Each took time in town to woo
A tantalizing fellow

Their fellows were red-headed flowers
Fit, fine and full of fun
Maribelle picked two to woo
Marigold picked one

They swept those fellows off their roots
With sweet talk, dance and song—
Would you have picked those flowers, too,
If you had gone along?

FULL MOON

Night on the verandah:
Across the bay
Village lights
Sprinkled on hills
Stripe the dark water

The silver round
Of the full moon
Slips into the cloud
As a coin
Slips into a purse

RAIN COMING

When a mermaid winks
Look for a shower
Children at the seashore
Splashing by the hour
See rain coming
Soaked as they can get
Cry, "Quick!
Duck under
So you don't get wet!"

THE BLACKBIRDS' PARTY

Birds like to party
I party, too
But not the way
The blackbirds do

Why all the fuss?
They party like us

Oh, blackbirds flap
They strut and peck
Right claw forward
Left claw back

How many in all
Having a ball?

Ten in the pool
Six on the grass
Cawing so cool
Like a birdland jazz

School of fish
Pool as a dish

Five dive under
To fish and sup
Smack their beaks
When they come up

So many to treat
What else did they eat?

After the fish
Ate worms for a snack
Right claw forward
Left claw back

VINE LEAVES

The farmer
Built firm frames
For vines
To climb
Now
A morning assembly
Of vine leaves
Boogies on down
The upright
Uptight
Trellis

MY DAD

When my dad
Blows his silver horn
Folks follow the music
Dance on in

Not saying
Nobody else
Can play sax
But my dad
Can play sax
Like nobody else

GOOD FLOWER BLUES

Pretty flowers bloomin',
Got flowers on my mind.
I see pretty flowers bloomin',
Gorgeous flowers on my mind.
When I looks out and sees 'em
Thanks God that I ain't blind.

My children went and picked 'em,
Put those flowers in a bowl.
Lord, my little children picked 'em,
Put those flowers in a bowl.
I'll feed my little children,
'Cause they knows what feeds my soul.

BEADED BRAIDS

After the brilliance
Of Carnival and sun,
Eyes ease,
Close
On shadows of rain.

The braided
Beaded lady
Restores soul-color,
Reminding me
Of photographs
In family albums
Patchwork pages
Of old friends:
Ancestral guardians.

The braided
Beaded lady
Smiles
Colors glow
Through quiet grays—
Remarkable.

THE HURRICANE

I cried to the wind,
"Don't blow so hard!
You've knocked down my sister
You're shaking
And tossing and tilting
The tree!"

And would the wind listen,
Listen to me?

The wind howled,
"*Whooree!*
I blow as I wish
I wish
I wish
I crush and
I splash and
I rush and
I swish."

I cried to the wind,
"Don't blow so wild!
You're chasing the clouds
You're whirling
And swishing and swirling
The sea!"

And would the wind listen,
Listen to me?

The wind howled,
"Whooree!
I blow as I wish
I wish
I wish
I'm bold and
I'm brash and
I'm cold and
I'm rash!"

I said to my friends,
"Please, call out with me,
Stop, wind, stop!"
   "STOP, WIND, STOP!"

Ah, *now* the wind listens
It brushes my hair
Chases clouds slowly
Sings in my ear,
"Whooree, whooree!"
Stretches out gently
Under the tree
Soothes little sister
And quiets the sea.

DO GOOD

Donkey want water
Birdies want food
Somebody ought to
Do them good

Birdies got a mama
Papa on the go
Bring them food and water
Feed them, too

Donkey tied proper
He holler, he bawl
No mama, no papa
To feed him at all

GRAPE PICKERS

Grape pickers singing
By a frangipani tree
Filled their pots and bellies
But they wouldn't fill me

Sang when they were merry
But when they were glum
    They wouldn't give a grape away
    You wouldn't ever hear them say,
"Dog have a bite!"
Or, "Cat, have some!"

LEAVING

There is always
A certain sadness to it
Leaving, leaving
Hoping to return

The plane rising
Above the tropical island

Mama at the gate fence
Looking up
Waving, waving

The plane disappears.

VILLAGE VOICES

No drums
No steel band tonight
Voices of the village
Outsinging all instruments

Like roots
Singing through tree trunks
Voices branch out
To leaves of melody

It is as if
Earth sings,
Trees sing,
Sky sings—
It is as if
In all the singing
This small island
Washed in ocean blues
Swims away

GRANNY

Granny had a way with fruit trees
Hear me now
She mixed fruit slices in her dough
Knew just how
When she wasn't busy in her kitchen
Baking bread
She balanced baskets with her produce
On her head

She filled her baskets with her fruitbread
Took her time
Put pawpaw, mango, pomegranate
Guava and lime
She sauntered to the village market
Easy pace
She stepped out better than a queen
Had more grace

But she'd sass you if you vexed her, mon
What I found
No car could move her out the road
Stood her ground
She'd turn and shake a fist and shout,
"Want a lickin'?
Mash me down, nuh
You t'ink me name chicken!"

THE ARTIST

I know a man
Like a child
He loves to paint
He can paint anything
He sets his heart to

He knows
That to have
Anything he loves
He can have it
Fair and forever
If he paints
A picture of it

He knows
That to face
Anything that hurts
He can do it
Transform the sorrow
If he paints
A picture of it

This is how he lives
This is what he does

PRETTY IS

When I say
The painting
Of the flower
Is pretty
The word "pretty"
Can't compare to the flower
Nor even to the picture
Of the flower

When I say
The painting
Of the flower
Is pretty
Pretty is
How good I feel
When I see it
And say it

THE FLOWER'S PERFUME

Listen my dear
It's not the way
You comb your hair
Part it
Or don't
For when you wear
A flower there
No one cares about your tresses
Or what color your dress is.

The flower's perfume
Fills the air
In the room
Or wherever you are
And its color
Sings
Brightening your eyes
So even in moonlight
I look at you and say,
"Good *morning!*"

STORYTELLER

Emerald
Grew up in flowers
Hibiscus, poinsettia, bougainvillea
Birds pieced her stories together
With song

She sheltered
Under stories
Tropical rains, lightning,
War of thunder
Couldn't disturb her

Later she told stories
To grandchildren
Backed by Gabriel's horn
Her words skirted thorns
Winged
Agile as birdsong
Dazzling as jazz

MAMA'S BOUQUETS

Sun every day
Heat year round
Mama sang
As she clipped flowers
In the garden
  Surprising butterflies
  And hummingbirds
Each day

Mama's bouquets
In every room
Sweetened
And brightened the air
Wherever we looked
Flowers
Indoors and out
Always

We are grown and gone
Our rooms are silent
Still
Mama sings
As she gathers flowers
  Surprising butterflies
  And hummingbirds
Each day

We say,
"Save your strength, Ma!"
We ask,
"Who sees bouquets
In empty rooms?"

Mama says,
"God is here
Always
With the flowers
And my song
Each day
When you are gone."

BIG QUESTIONS

Jawara
Asks big questions
Like,
Does a baby
Think in words
Before it can talk?

He knows
He's always been here
He and his sister, Ashaki

He wonders
About mothers and fathers
And children

He asks,
Dad,
Before you and Mom
Got married
Did me and my sister
Live together
All alone
By ourselves?

TASTE THE AIR

My little brother's legs
Are springs
The way he bounces.
  No walk step
  In him,
  He jumps
  Tastes air
  Laughs—
He goes
After goats
Prancing over the wall
Into the garden.
  How those goats
  Worry the hibiscus!
  They find it
  Delicious.
Little brother
Leaps
"POM-PA-LOM!"
He shouts.
  I laugh at the sight.
  See them there?
  Goats, hibiscus, boy—
  Dancing!

ANCESTRY

I splash in the ocean
My big brother watches me
We sing,
   "Wade in the water
   Wade in the water, children."

Mom and Dad
Teaching us spirituals
Reading us African tales
Singing songs
Telling stories
Reminding us
Of our ancestry

On the beach
Other children
Dig to China
I dig
To Africa